GHOST GHOUL & ZOMBIE JOKES

Tyler Stewart

QUAGMIRE PRESS

Ghoul Jokes

Q: Who was the ghoul's favorite dancer?
A: The boogieman!

Q: Which ghoul runs the city?
A: The night-mayor!

Q: Why was the ghoul taken to prison?
A: Because he was ghoulty of a crime!

Q: Who did Frankenstein take to the prom?
A: His ghoulfriend!

Q: What can't you sell to a ghoul?
A: Life insurance!

Q: What should you do with a blue ghoul?
A: Try to cheer it up!

3

More Ghoul Jokes

Q: Why couldn't the witch and ghoul go to school together?
A: Because the ghoul couldn't spell!

Q: What is a ghoul's favorite pet?
A: His ghouldfish!

Q: What do people say about the ghoul with six arms?
A: He's very handy!

Q: How many ghouls does it take to change a light bulb?
A: None, they don't need light!

Q: When do ghouls cook their victims?
A: On Fry Day!

Q: Do ghouls eat candy with their fingers?
A: No, they eat the fingers separately!

Still More Ghoul Jokes

Q: What is a ghoul's
favorite flavour?
A: Lemon and slime!

Q: Why do
ghouls and demons
get along well?
A: Because demons
are a ghoul's
best friend!

Q: How did the
ghoul get
so smart?
A: By always
eating brains!

Q: What is so light it can float on air?
A: A ghoul's brain!

Q: Why did the teacher kick my dead friend out of class?
A: Because he's too ghoul for school!

Q: What did uncle ghoul say to his nephew?
A: You gruesome since last I saw you!

Even More Ghoul Jokes

Q: Why did the
ghoul slurp
his food?
A: Because he was
a goblin!

Q: What happened
to the green ghoul?
A: It was sick of
eating brains!

Q: Why did
the ghoul eat
a light bulb?
A: Because he
wanted
a light snack!

8

Q: What do ghosts say when something is awesome?
A: That's really ghoul!

Q: What is in the ghoul's favorite hotel?
A: Rot and mold in every room!

Q: What made the ghoul a winner?
A: He kicked the game winning field ghoul!

Ghost Jokes

Q: What is a pirate ghost's drink of choice?
A: Boo-tea!

Q: How do ghosts get ghouls' attention?
A: They wooooo them!

BOO

Q: What is a ghost's favorite greeting?
A: How do you boo?!

Q: What kind of key does a ghost use?
A: A spoo-key!

Q: What do ghosts tell their children?
A: Only spook when spoken too!

Q: What do ghosts drink to wake up?
A: Coffee with scream and sugar!

More Ghost Jokes

Q: Why did the game warden give the ghost a ticket?
A: The ghost didn't have a haunting license!

Q: What did the ghost ask the other ghost?
A: Do you believe in humans?!

Q: Why didn't the ghost go to the party?
A: He had no body to go with!

Q: Why are ghosts bad liars?
A: Because you can see right through them!

Q: Why do ghosts ride elevators?
A: To raise their spirits!

Still More Ghost Jokes

EAT
Drink
and
BE
SCARY

Q: What is the ghost's motto?
A: Eat, drink and be scary!

Q: What did the ghost get when it scraped its knee?
A: A boo-boo!

Q: How do you tell if a ghost is sad?
A: He starts boo hooing!

Q: Where does a ghost get food?
A: The ghost-ry store!

Q: How does a ghost build muscle?
A: By exorcising daily!

Q: What do you call a ghost with a broken leg?
A: A hoblin goblin!

15

Even More Ghost Jokes

Q: What is in
a ghost's nose?
A: Boo-gers!

Q: Which ghosts
hear best?
A: The eeriest!

Q: Why did the
ghost go to the
Boxing Day sales?
A: Because he's
a bargain haunter!

Q: What is a ghosts favorite theme park ride?
A: The roller-ghoster!

Q: Where do ghosts go on holiday?
A: The Boohamas or Maliboo!

Q: Why don't ghosts eat candy?
A: They have no stomach for it!

Zombie Jokes

Q: What do you call a zombie without a mind?
A: Hungry!

Q: Why couldn't the zombie get a job as a chef?
A: Because his cooking was rotten!

Q: What makes a great zombie?
A: Dead-ication!

Q: What do you call a zombie that can't run?
A: The walking dead!

Q: Why did the zombie stay home from school?
A: He felt rotten!

Q: Why did the zombie become an undertaker?
A: To put food on the table!

More Zombie Jokes

Q: Can zombies be arrested?
A: No, you'll never take them alive!

GNAW BONE
PRISON
690646

Q: Why was the zombie left-handed?
A: Because his right arm fell right off!

What kind of food do zombies hate the most?
A: Fast food!

Q: Why did the zombie join the army?
A: Because they give out arms!

Q: How do you know if a zombie likes a person?
A: They ask for seconds!

Q: Why did the zombie cross the road?
A: To eat the chicken!

Still More Zombie Jokes

Q: Where do zombies relax?
A: The unliving room!

Q: How much does it cost to feed a zombie?
A: An arm and a leg!

Q: What did the zombie get his girlfriend for Valentine's Day?
A: A box of brains and a deady bear!

Q: What did the zombie make when it got into the wrong tomb?
A: A grave mistake!

Q: What do dyslexic zombies eat?
A: Brians!

Q: What do zombies do at a wedding?
A: Toast the bride and groom!

Even More Zombie Jokes

Q: What's another name for a vegetarian zombie?
A: Liar!

Q: What do zombies do about bad breath?
A: They chew on some Flesh Mint!

Q: What is a lame
joke told by
a zombie?
A: A groaner!

Q: What is the
worst thing to
give a zombie?
A: A piece of
your mind!

Q: What is a zombie's
favorite greeting?
A: Nice to eat you!

Q: Why did the
zombie go to
the dentist?
A: To improve his bite!

25

General Monster Jokes

Q: On what street do monsters live?
A: A Skull-de-sac!

Q: What do you get when you cross ghouls with humans?
A: Zombies!

Q: Which monster enjoys dancing?
A: A boogieman!

Q: How did the monster predict her future?
A: With her horror-scope!

Q: Who's a monster's favorite family member?
A: Their mummy!

Q: What is the best way to speak to a ghoul, ghost or zombie?
A: From far away!

Halloween Jokes

Q: Why do children like Halloween?
A: Because it is pretty ghoul!

Q: What should you do if hundreds of ghouls, ghosts and zombies surround your house?
A: Hope it's Halloween!

Q: What should you do if a zombie rolls its eyes at you at a Halloween party?
A: Roll them back!

Q: Who did the boy ghost take to the Halloween dance?
A: His bootiful ghoulfriend!

Q: What is a ghoul's favorite colour of Halloween candy?
A: Green, it matches their skin!

Q: What is a baby ghost's favorite Halloween costume?
A: A pillowcase!

School Jokes

Q: Why did the monster get an F on his essay? A: Because he plague-gerized it!

Q: Where do parents send their ghoul children? A: Skghoul!

Q: What happened to the ghoul who failed the test?
A: The teacher scghoulded him!

Q: Where do young ghouls go after school?
A: To after school-scare!

Q: What did the ghost teacher tell the class?
A: Look at the board, and I will go through it again!

Sports Jokes

Q: Why did the zombie eat the archer?
A: He wanted his bone and marrow!

Q: What does a zombie say before a boxing match?
A: Do you want a piece of me?!

Q: What position does a ghoul play in soccer?
A: Ghoulie!

Q: Why did the zombie pitcher quit baseball?
A: He threw his arm out!

Q: How do monsters clean the ice between periods at the hockey game?
A: With a zombie-oni!

Q: What's a ghoul's favorite sport?
A: A nice round of ghoulf!

33

Place Jokes

Q: Where is a ghost's favorite place in the United States?
A: North and South Scarolina!

Q: Where do zombies vacation?
A: The Deaditerranean!

Q: What is a monster's favorite lake?
A: Lake Eerie!

Q: When did all the ghouls head to California?
A: During the ghould-rush!

Q: Where do hockey's Oilers play?
A: Deadmonton, Alberta, Canada

Q: Where do monsters go for a swim?
A: The Dead Sea!

Game Jokes

Q: What is a Zombie's favorite game?
A: Chase!

Q: What kind of ghost plays cards?
A: A polkergeist!

Q: What is a monster's favorite game show?
A: Chomping on the Stars!

Q: What is a ghost's favorite party game?
A: Hide and Go Shriek!

Q: Why did the girl ghosts have a game night?
A: Because ghouls just want to have fun!

Animal Jokes

Q: What do you call zombies with yellow and black stripes?
A: Zom-bees!

ZOMBEES

Q: What does a zombie rabbit do?
A: Hare-raising!

Q: What did the ghost of a panda eat?
A: Bam-boo!

Q: Where do you find zombie monkeys?
A: The brain forest!

Q: What do you get when you cross owls with ghosts?
A: Something that scares you and doesn't give a hoot!

Q: Who is a Ghoul's best friend?
A: A Ghoulden Retriever!

Art-sy Jokes

Q: Who is a ghost's favorite detective?
A: Sherlock Moans!

Q: What is a ghoul's favorite play?
A: Romeo and Ghouliet!

Q: Why did the zombie start eating sheet music?
A: Because it was de-composing!

Q: How do you write a very scary book?
A: With a ghostwriter!

Q: What did a ghost see in a theatre?
A: A phantomine!

Technology Jokes

Q: How does a ghost pay for dinner?
A: With crypto-currency!

Q: How do you like a post on zombie-book?
A: Click the "Bite Me" button!

Q: What do zombies read on news sites?
A: The HEADlines!

Q: What is a ghoul's email signature?
A: Best witches and worm regards!

Q: What is a ghoul's favorite search engine?
A: Ghoulgle!

Q: Why was the computer scary?
A: It had terrorbytes of information!

Cemetery Jokes

Q: Why was there a fence around the cemetery?
A: Because people were dying to get in!

Q: What is a zombie sleepover?
A: A mass grave!

Q: Why was the
zombie gravedigger fired?
A: He buried someone
in the wrong hole,
a grave mistake!

Q: Why did the zombie
bury his prized trophy?
A: Because he wanted
it enGRAVED!

Q: What are
a monster's
favorite trees?
A: Ceme-trees!

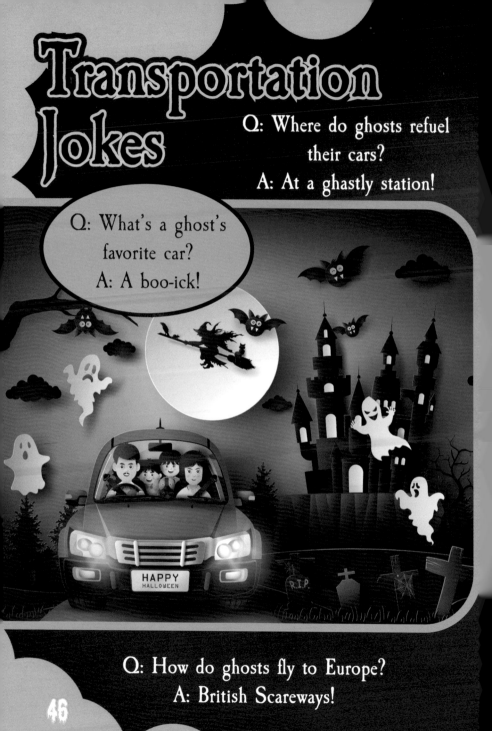

Q: What do ghosts use to fly long distances?
A: A scareplane!

Q: What is the dream vehicle for a zombie?
A: A monster truck!

Party Jokes

Q: What do ghosts do at dance parties?
A: Boogie down!

Q: Who did the zombie avoid eating at the party?
A: The clown, it tasted funny!

Q: Who did the zombie invite to his party?
A: Anyone he could dig up!

Q: How does a zombie greet you at a dinner party?
A: "Pleased to eat you, my dear!"

Q: What do ghosts do at sleepover parties?
A: Tell scary human stories!

49

Food Jokes

Q: What's a monster's favorite drink?
A: Ghoul-Aid!

Q: What do college ghouls and zombies eat?
A: Raw-men!

Q: What is a ghoul's favorite chocolate?
A: Hearse-sheys!

Q: What is ghoul and zombie's favorite pizza topping?
A: Ghost Peppers!

Q: What is a zombie's favorite cheese?
A: Zom-brie!

Q: What do you call a zombie that eats a lot of breakfast?
A: A cereal killer!

More Food Jokes

Q: What is a zombie's favorite food?
A: You!

Q: When do ghosts eat breakfast?
A: In the moaning; at ATE O'clock!

Q: What is a zombie's least favorite candy?
A: A Life Saver!

Q: Who does a ghoul go to for their favorite cookies? A: The ghoul-scouts!

Q: What is a zombie's favorite type of bean? A: A human bean!

Q: What do zombies like on their fries? A: Grave-y!

Sir
F. Rench Fry

Always Best
with
Grave-y

Paris
1775-1789

Still More Food Jokes

Q: What is a zombie's favorite bread?
A: Whole brain!

Q: Why do zombies hang around Subway?
A: So they can Eat Flesh!

Q: What do monsters eat for supper?
A: Ghoulash!

Q: What is a ghost's favorite dessert?
A: I-scream and booberry pie!

Q: How do ghosts like their eggs cooked?
A: Terror-fried!

Q: What is a ghost's favorite food?
A: Hamboogers and flies!

Monsterly Attire Jokes

Q: What is a well dressed Zombie?
A: Dressed to kill!

Q: What is a zombie's favorite makeup?
A: Mas-scare-a!

Q: What do ghouls and zombies use to do their hair?

A: Scare-spray!

Q: What kind of tie does a ghost wear to a formal party?

A: A boo-tie!

Weather Jokes

Q: What do ghoul werewolves do when it is a full moon?
A: They ghowl!

Q: What does a monster wear on its feet in the rain?
A: Ghoul-oshes!

Q: What happened to the ghost that was lost in the fog?
A: He was mist!

Q: What is a zombie's favorite weather?
A: B-rain!

Q: Why do ghosts hate rain?
A: Because it dampens their spirits!

Little Monster Jokes

Q: What do you call the smallest zombie?
A: Tomb Thumb!

Q: What do you call a little ghost's mom and dad?
A: Transparents!

Q: How do young monsters travel in the morning?
A: They ride the scghoul bus!

Q: What do you call little zombie twins?
A: Dead ringers!

Q: What do you call a child ghost with a tear in its sheet?
A: A hole-y terror!

SCHOOL BUS

Monster Health Jokes

Q: How do you know a zombie is sick?
A: It coffins and groans!

Q: Why did people stop going to the ghoul hospital?
A: They kept coming out dead!

Q: Why did the zombie visit the hospital?
A: He wanted to learn some sick jokes!

Q: Why did the ghost make a doctor's appointment?
A: To get a boo-ster shot!

Q: Why did the zombie get rushed to a hospital?
A: Because his condition was grave!

The Publisher: Quagmire Press Ltd.

Website: www.quagmirepress.com

Library and Archives Canada Cataloguing in Publication

Title: Ghost, ghoul & zombie jokes / Tyler Stewart.

Other titles: Ghost, ghoul and zombie jokes

Names: Stewart, Tyler, author.

Identifiers: Canadiana (print) 20220192553 | Canadiana (ebook) 20220192588 | ISBN 9781926695532 (softcover) | ISBN 9781926695549 (PDF)

Subjects: LCSH: Monsters—Humor. | LCGFT: Humor.

Classification: LCC PN6231.M665 S74 2022 | DDC jC818/.602—dc23

Project Director: Hank Boer

Project Editor: Wendy Pirk

Design & Layout: Ryschell Dragunov

Front cover: Getty Images: Cattallina, memoangeles, NeoLeo, sabelskaya

Back cover: Getty Images: Cattallina, sabelskaya, ia_64, sararoom, ALINA, TatianaNikulina, NeoLeo

PhotoCredits: Getty Images: Dualororua, 48; solar22, 36; betoon, 16; Evgenia Ponomareva, 62; Tigatelu, 63; Iuliia Bessonova, 60; MOMOKO TAKEUCHI, 60; Dimitry Mirolyubov, 59; PenWin, 56; artestworks, 55; Samuil_Levich, 54; Btownchris, 53; osker, 52; cthoman, 52; GreenArtPhotography, 51; AngalR3ind, 50; Khaneeros, 49; shock77, 47; Larysa Amosova, 44; passigatti, 41; Tomacco, 40; coolgraphic, 40; wowwa, 38; warawiri, 39; branca_escova, 36; memoangeles, 2, 21, 28, 35; artestworks, 33, 24; woocat, 13, ZeSaiphio Design, 1, 53, 55, 58; IvanNikulin, 62; Catya_Shok, 61; colematt, 61; FOTOKITA, 59; Umkarra, 57; Luiza Nalimova, 56; Fudio, 54; zwfirchik06, 5; Digital Vision, 48; S-E-R-G-O, 49; Chalabala, 47; thanaphiphat, 46; il67, 45; AtomStudios, 45; Lilken, 44; BrianAJackson, 43; CNuisin, 26; Anastasia Boriagina, 19; mutsMaks, 32; toonerman, 33; Julia Pavaliuk, 15; Heorhii Aryshtevych, 15; Ieta, 14; Darijashka, 14; McIninch, 12; ChrisGorgio, 9; DesignWolf, 9; klyaksun, 8; Julia Neroznak, 10; Darko Mlinarevic , 10; PaulMichaelHughes., 8; ia_64, 7; wowomnom, 7; alenaohneva, 6; djvstock, 5; IgorZakowski, 4; julos, 5; Deklofenak, 4; Ryan Rad, 34; Drawkman, 35; Mark Murphy, 2; Dantyya, 6; GB_Art, 34; Anton Dzyna, 16; Ieta, 14; ChrisGorgio, 32; Caratti, 17; monkeybusinessimages, 17; joey333, 22; Madmaxer, 42; hjalmeida, 31; Alefclipart, 22; Eisenlohr, 23; 3dalia, 31; ralbornoz, 11; SeventyFour, 28; Sudowoodo, 43; Ricky Saputra, 38; IcemanJ, 30; shin28, 41; yayayoyo, 25; serazetdinov, 29; IconicBestiary, 37; Irina Kashaeva, 39; yayayoyo, 23; sararoom, 18; Irina Cheremisinova, 3; wildpixel, 24; antonbrand, 21; angkritth, 42; 3dalia, 19; losw, 20; Denis-Art, 26; amandasmith, 27; Seven tyFour, 30; shironosov, 27; SurfUpVector, 29; Muhammad Aditya Hanafi, 18; brue, 13; Ilya Okty, 55; Tetiana Lazunova ,12; Dualororua, 58; melazerg, 50.

Produced with the assistance of the Government of Alberta.

Alberta

Government

Printed in China

PC: 38-1